USBORNE

1001
Things to spot
on
Holiday

Hazel Maskell

Illustrated by Teri Gower

Additional design by Nelupa Hussain
Edited by Anna Milbourne

Contents

Things to spot

This book shows holiday scenes from all around the world. In each big picture there are lots of things for you to find and count.

There is a puzzle on pages 30 to 31 with even more things to find throughout the book. There are 1001 things to spot altogether.

Coral-reef diving

8 yellow flippers
9 cleaner wrasse
8 clownfish
10 angelfish
4 blue sea stars
7 Moorish idols
10 snappers
1 zebra shark
2 octopuses
9 blue damselfish

16

Each little picture shows you what to look for in the big picture.

The number tells you how many of that thing you need to find.

Alex loves going on holiday, and she's heading off on a long trip all around the world. Can you spot her in each of the big pictures?

Plane trip

5 flowery shirts

8 eyemasks

2 straw hats

7 trays of food

9 cushions

6 cans of fizzy orange

10 sets of headphones

3 spotty suitcases

8 safety cards

9 puzzle books

Water park

3 lifeguards 4 waiters 9 ice-cream sundaes 8 straw parasols 10 yellow armbands

5 life rings
2 pirate flags
9 green swimming caps
7 toy dolphins
10 sunloungers

Beach party

9 flower garlands

10 glasses of punch

8 cobs of corn

9 slices of watermelon

3 yachts

7 steel drums

6 beach balls

1 ice-cream cake

8 palm trees

10 paper lanterns

Amusement park

4 fairy princesses

6 dragon cars

10 tubs of ice cream

9 picnic tables

10 bears marching

2 haunted trains

10 giant spiders

8 toy dogs

9 star balloons

4 logs

At the ranch

1 main lodge

6 foals

7 brown horses

8 backpacks

10 butterflies

12

9 water bottles

5 coyotes

8 jays

6 ranch cats

10 brown-and-white cows

Coral-reef diving

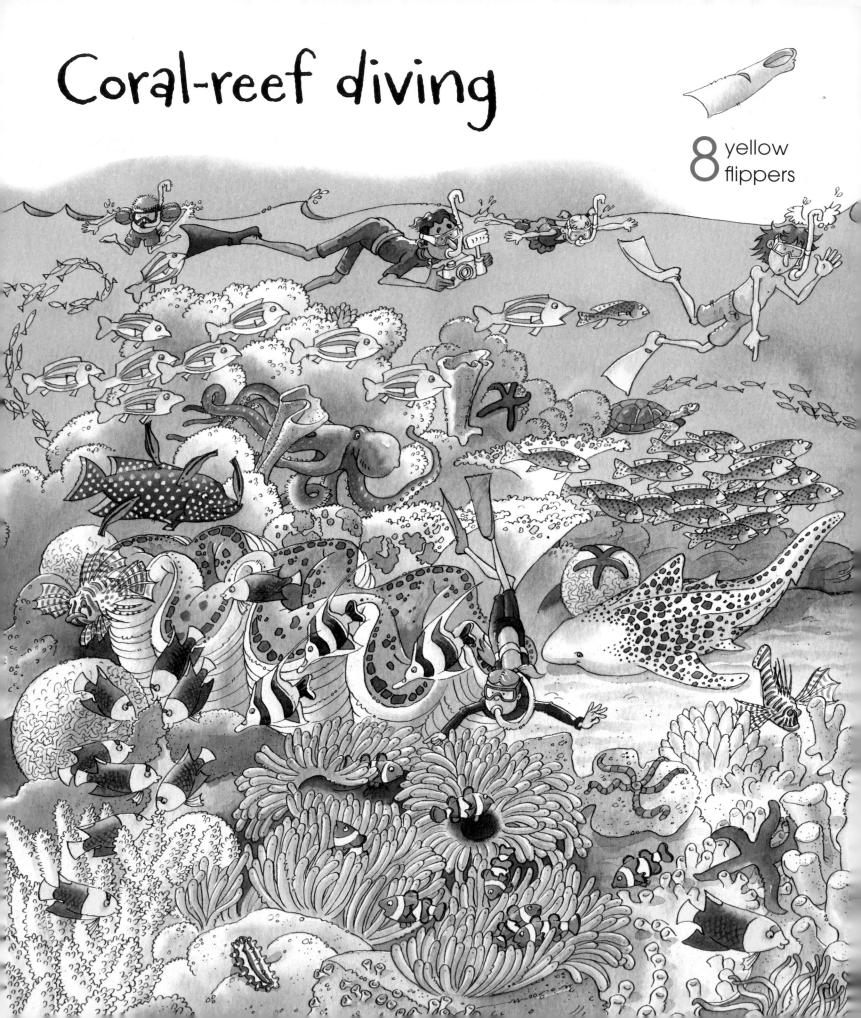

8 yellow flippers

9 cleaner wrasse

8 clownfish

10 angelfish

4 blue sea stars

7 Moorish idols

10 snappers

1 zebra shark

2 octopuses

9 blue damselfish

Summer camp

5 log cabins   **4** archery targets   **9** climbing helmets   **7** chipmunks   **8** basketballs

10 paddles

6 canoes

10 painted plates

9 ducks

3 trampolines

Whale-watching tour

10 dolphins   **7** portholes   **6** seals   **1** captain   **9** gannets

7 waterproof jackets

8 cormorants

1 whale tail

7 seagulls

6 fishing boats

On the ski slopes

9 snowboards

10 mugs of hot chocolate

3 snowmen

6 red poles

6 chairlifts

3 parasols

4 strings of lights

7 hungry birds

10 pink ski goggles

20

8 striped scarves

Carnival parade

7 tambourines

3 giant flowers

10 yellow pompoms

4 men on stilts

2 pink headdresses

10 tall hats

5 juggling clowns

7 elves

3 parasols

4 jesters

On safari

10 zebras

6 lion cubs

8 weaver birds' nests

10 meerkats

7 hyenas

3 baby elephants

9 antelope

4 termite mounds

5 khaki hats

2 jeeps

25

Camping

5 green tents

7 chicken drumsticks

8 pancakes

10 plates of beans

5 drums

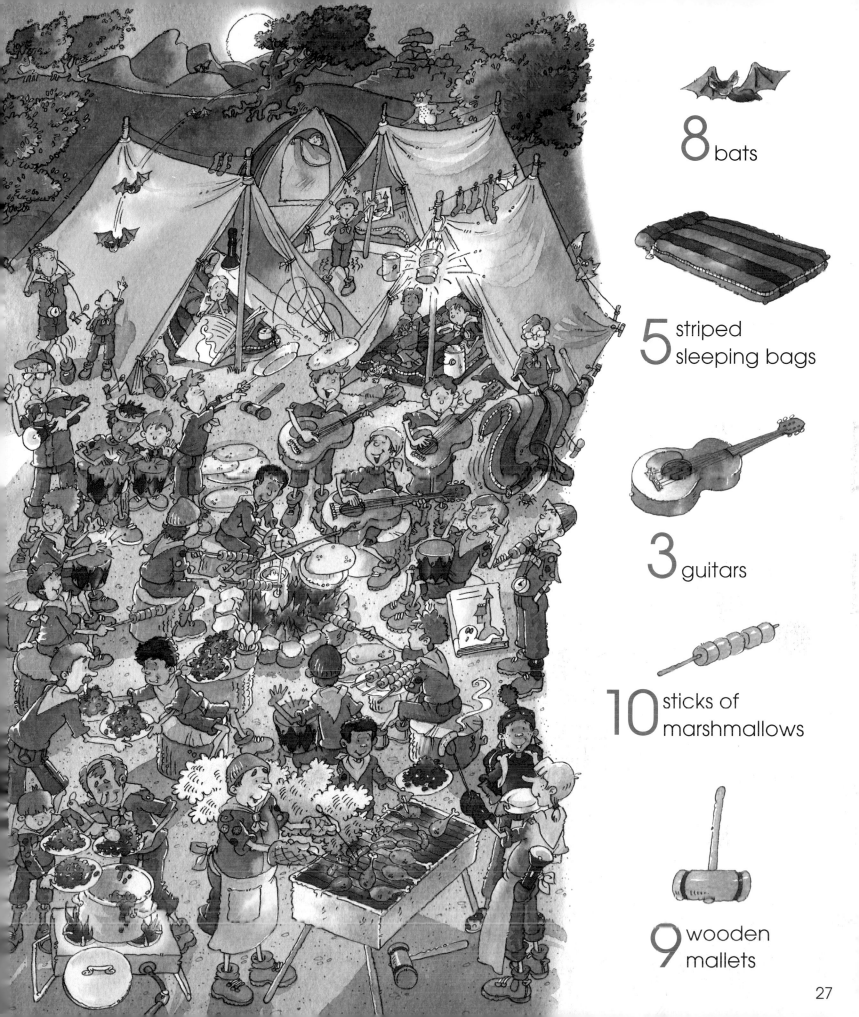

8 bats

5 striped sleeping bags

3 guitars

10 sticks of marshmallows

9 wooden mallets

Winter wonderland

8 snowshoes   5 huskies   6 squirrels   7 red-and-white hats   9 reindeer

6 yellow sleds   **5** trees with lights   **9** lanterns   **4** harnesses with bells   **10** swans

Airport shop

Alex is at the airport shop, looking for souvenirs. There are lots of things for sale that could be useful on different kinds of holidays. Look back through the book to see if you can find and count them all.

6 sets of binoculars

9 blue-and-white caps

6 books of ghost stories

8 magazines

10 hats with stars

8 striped towels

9 cowboy hats

6 boxes of pencils

10 guidebooks

6 white diving masks

4 underwater cameras

6 compasses

8 sets of earmuffs

7 seahorse T-shirts

6 packs of cards

7 swirly lollipops

Answers

Did you find all the things from the airport shop?
Here's where they all are:

6 sets of binoculars
On safari
(pages 24-25)

9 blue-and-white caps
Whale-watching tour
(pages 18-19)

6 books of ghost stories
Camping
(pages 26-27)

8 magazines
Summer camp
(pages 16-17)

10 hats with stars
On the ski slopes
(pages 20-21)

8 striped towels
Water park
(pages 6-7)

9 cowboy hats
At the ranch
(pages 12-13)

6 boxes of pencils
Plane trip
(pages 4-5)

10 guidebooks
Amusement park
(pages 10-11)

6 white diving masks
Coral-reef diving
(pages 14-15)

4 underwater cameras
Coral-reef diving
(pages 14-15)

6 compasses
Camping
(pages 26-27)

8 sets of earmuffs
Winter wonderland
(pages 28-29)

7 seahorse T-shirts
Beach party
(pages 8-9)

6 packs of cards
Plane trip
(pages 4-5)

7 swirly lollipops
Carnival parade
(pages 22-23)

With thanks to Drs. Margaret and John Rostron for advice about wildlife.
With special thanks to Nick Wakeford and Ian McNee for help in completing the artwork.

First published in 2011 by Usborne Publishing Ltd.,
Usborne House, 83-85 Saffron Hill, London EC1N 8RT, England. www.usborne.co.uk